Karl Marx

Quotes... Vol.12

by The Secret Libraries

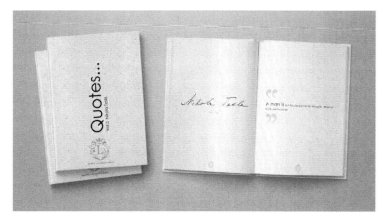

Kindle EDITION

The Secret Libraries

Published by The Secret Libraries
www.thesecretlibraries.com
Annotation and Artists Background by The Secret Libraries 2016

Paperback:
ISBN-13: 978-1540637178
ISBN-10: 1540637174

Quotes...

This book provides a selected collection of 201 quotes from the works of Karl Marx.

Karl Marx

1818-1883

The oppressed are allowed once every few years to decide which particular representatives of the oppressing class are to represent and repress them.

The philosophers have only interpreted the world, in various ways. The point, however, is to change it.

Surround yourself with people who make you happy. People who make you laugh, who help you when you're in need. People who genuinely care. They are the ones worth keeping in your life. Everyone else is just passing through.

The last capitalist we hang shall be the one who sold us the rope.

Hegel remarks somewhere that all great, world-historical facts and personages occur, as it were, twice. He has forgotten to add: the first time as tragedy, the second as farce.

Reason has always existed, but not always in a reasonable form.

Men make their own history, but they do not make it as they please; they do not make it under self-selected circumstances, but under circumstances existing already, given and transmitted from the past.

I **am** nothing but I must be everything.

Let the ruling classes tremble at a Communistic revolution. The proletarians have nothing to lose but their chains. They have a world to win. Workingmen of all countries unite!

Go on, get out! Last words are for fools who haven't said enough!

We call communism the real movement which abolishes the present state of things. The conditions of this movement result from the premises now in existence.

Just as man is governed, in religion, by the products of his own brain, so, in capitalist production, he is governed by the products of his own hand.

Great progress was evident in the last Congress of the American 'Labour Union' in that among other things, it treated working women with complete equality...Anybody who knows anything of history knows that great social changes are impossible without the feminine ferment.

The less

you eat, drink and read books; the less you go to the theatre, the dance hall, the public house; the less you think, love, theorize, sing, paint, fence, etc., the more you save-the greater becomes your treasure which neither moths nor dust will devour-your capital.

"

To be radical is to grasp things by the root.

"

The bourgeoisie cannot exist without constantly revolutionizing the instruments of production, and thereby the relations of production, and with them the whole relations of society.

It is not the consciousness of men that determines their being, but, on the contrary, their social being that determines their consciousness.

The ideas of the ruling class are in every epoch the ruling ideas, i.e. the class which is the ruling material force of society, is at the same time its ruling intellectual force.

The bourgeoisie, by the rapid improvement of all instruments of production, by the immensely facilitated means of communication, draws all, even the most barbarian nations into civilization.

If anything is certain, it is that I myself am not a Marxist.

Religion is the impotence of the human mind to deal with occurrences it cannot understand.

In proportion therefore, as the repulsiveness of the work increases, the wage decreases.

Communism is the riddle of history solved, and it knows itself to be this solution.

There is no royal road to science, and only those who do not dread the fatiguing climb of its steep paths have a chance of gaining its luminous summits.

But modern bourgeois private property is the final and most complete expression of the system of producing and appropriating products, that is based on class antagonisms, on the exploitation of the many by the few.

Society does not consist of individuals, but expresses the sum of interrelations, the relations within which these individuals stand.

Then the world will be for the common people, and the sounds of happiness will reach the deepest springs. Ah! Come! People of every land, how can you not be roused.

You are horrified at our intending to do away with private property. But in your existing society private property is already done away with for nine-tenths of the population; its existence for the few is solely due to its non-existence in the hands of those nine-tenths.

Communism deprives no man of the power to appropriate the products of society: all that it does is to deprive him of the power to subjugate the labor of others by means of such appropriation.

The education of all children, from the moment that they can get along without a mother's care, shall be in state institutions.

Religion is the sigh of the oppressed creature, the heart of a heartless world and the soul of soulless conditions. It is the opium of the people.

Labor in the white skin can never free itself as long as labor in the black skin is branded.

The increase in value of the world of things is directly proportional to the decrease in value of the human world.

Moments are the elements of profit.

A commodity appears at first sight an extremely obvious, trivial thing. But its analysis brings out that it is a very strange thing, abounding in metaphysical subtleties and theological niceties.

Education is

free. Freedom of education shall be enjoyed under the condition fixed by law and under the supreme control of the state.

If you love without evoking love in return - if through the vital expression of yourself as a loving person you fail to become a loved person, then your love is impotent, it is a misfortune.

The ruling ideas of each age have ever been the ideas of its ruling class.

Accumulate, accumulate! This is Moses and the Prophets!

Money is the universal, self-constituted value of all things. Hence it has robbed the whole world... of its proper value. Money is the alienated essence of man's labour and life, and this alien essence dominates him as he worships it.

Capitalism: Teach a man to fish, but the fish he catches aren't his. They belong to the person paying him to fish, and if he's lucky, he might get paid enough to buy a few fish for himself.

It is well known how the monks wrote silly lives of Catholic Saints over the manuscripts on which the classical works of ancient heathendom had been written.

Necessity is blind until it becomes conscious. Freedom is the consciousness of necessity.

You must be aware that the reward for labour, and quantity of labour, are quite disparate things.

It has resolved personal worth into exchange value, and in place of numberless indefeasible chartered freedoms, it has set up that single, unconscionable freedom -- free trade. In one word, for exploitation, veiled by religious and political illusions, it has substituted naked, shameless, direct, brutal exploitation.

Once the inner connection is grasped, all theoretical belief in the permanent necessity of existing conditions collapses before their collapse in practice.

Such a crises occurs only where the ever-lengthening chain of payments, and an artificial system of settling them, has been fully developed.

Language is as old as consciousness, language is practical, real consciousness that exists for other men as well, and only therefore does it also exist for me; language, like consciousness, only arises from the need, the necessity, of intercourse with other men.

The theory of Communists may be summed up in the single sentence: Abolition of private property.

In reality, the laborer belongs to capital before he has sold himself to capital.

Our epoch, the epoch of the bourgeoisie, possesses, however, this distinct feature: it has simplified class antagonisms.

...it is all the more clear what we have to accomplish at present: I am referring to ruthless criticism of all that exists, ruthless both in the sense of not being afraid of the results it arrives at and in the sense of being just as little afraid of conflict with the powers that be.

Both for the production on a mass scale of this communist consciousness, and for the success of the cause itself, the alteration of men on a mass scale is necessary, an alteration which can only take place in a practical movement, a revolution; this revolution is necessary, therefore, not only because the ruling class cannot be overthrown in any other way, but also because the class overthrowing it can only in a revolution succeed in ridding itself of all the muck of ages and become fitted to found society anew.

Man makes his own history, but he does not make it out of the whole cloth; he does not make it out of conditions chosen by himself, but out of such as he finds close at hand.

The modern bourgeois society that has sprouted from the ruins of feudal society has not done away with class antagonisms. It has but established new classes, new conditions of oppression, new forms of struggle in place of the old ones.

As individuals express their life, so they are.

"

I am a machine condemned to devour books.

"

Merely quantitative differences, beyond a certain point, pass into qualitative changes.

Machinery which is not used is not capital.

The theoretical conclusions of the Communists are

in no way based on ideas or principles that have been invented, or discovered, by this or that would -be universal reformer. They merely express, in general terms, actual relations springing from an existing class struggle, from a historical movement going on under our very eyes.

Criticism has plucked the imaginary flowers on the chain not in order that man shall continue to bear that chain without fantasy or consolation, but so that he shall throw off the chain and pluck the living flower.

All mysteries which lead theory to mysticism find their rational solution in human practice and in the comprehension of this practice.

In fact, the proposition that man's species nature is estranged from him means that one man is estranged from the other, as each of them is from man's essential nature.

The bourgeois sees in his wife a mere instrument of production.

Within the capitalist system all methods for raising the social productiveness of labour are brought about at the cost of the individual labourer.

The economic structure of capitalist society has grown out of the economic structure of feudal society. The dissolution of the latter set free the elements of the former ...

These labourers, who must sell themselves piece-meal, are a commodity, like every other article of commerce, and are consequently exposed to all the vicissitudes of competition, to all the fluctuations of the market.

Nobody — not even "a musician of the future" — can live upon future products.

Atheism ... reminds one of children, assuring everyone who is ready to listen to them that they are not afraid of the bogy man.

Ignorance never yet helped anybody.

All science would be superfluous if the outward appearance and the essence of things directly coincided.

Capital is dead labour, which, vampire-like, lives only by sucking living labour, and lives the more, the more labour it sucks.

Each step in the development of the bourgeoisie was accompanied by a corresponding political advance in that class.

"

The production of too many useful things results in too many useless people.

"

Hitherto men have always formed wrong ideas about

themselves, about what they are and what they ought to be. They have arranged their relations according to their ideas of God, of normal man, etc. The products of their brains have got out of their hands. They, the creators, have bowed down before their creations.

The true law of economics is chance, and we learned people arbitrarily seize on a few moments and establish them as laws.

Communism deprives no man of the power to appropriate the products of society; all that it does is to deprive him of the power to subjugate the labour of others by means of such appropriation.

Every emancipation is a restoration of the human world and of human relationships to man himself.

Political power, properly so called, is merely the organised power of one class for oppressing another.

Society as a whole is more and more splitting up into two great hostile camps.

Everyone of our relationships with nature and man must be a definite expression of our real, individual life.

National differences and antagonisms between peoples are daily more and more vanishing, owing to the development of the bourgeoisie, to freedom of commerce, to the world-market, to uniformity in the mode of production and in the conditions of life corresponding thereto. The supremacy of the proletariat will cause them to vanish still faster.

Philosophers have hitherto only interpreted the world in various ways; the point, however, is to change it.

Self-contempt is a serpent that ever gnaws at one's breath, sucking the life-blood from one's own heart and mixing it with the poison of misanthropy and despair.

Wages are a direct consequence of estranged labor, and estranged labor is the direct cause of private property.

Every opinion based on scientific criticism I welcome.

The tradition of past generations weighs like the Alps on the brains of the living.

The present struggle between the South and North is, therefore, nothing but a struggle between two social systems, the system of slavery and the system of free labour. The struggle has broken out because the two systems can no longer live peacefully side by side on the North American continent. It can only be ended by the victory of one system or the other.

..."

...it happens that "society is saved" as often as the circle of its ruling class is narrowed, as often as a more exclusive interest asserts itself over the general.

""

When a great social revolution shall have mastered the results of the bourgeois epoch, the market of the world and the modern powers of production, and subjected them to the common control of the most advanced peoples, then only will human progress cease to resemble that hideous, pagan idol, who would not drink the nectar but from the skulls of the slain.

"

The first requisite for the happiness of the people is the abolition of religion.

"

> **The new era** differs from the old chiefly in that the lash begins to imagine itself possessed of genius.

Philosophy, as long as a drop of blood shall pulse in its world-subduing and absolutely free heart, will never grow tired of answering its adversaries with the cry of Epicurus: "Not the man who denies the gods worshiped by the multitude, but he who affirms of the gods what the multitude believes about them, is truly impious"

In a rational state it would be more appropriate to ensure that a cobbler passed an examination than an executive civil servant; because shoe-making is a craft in the absence of which it is still possible to be a good citizen and a man in society.

Private property has made us so stupid and one-sided that an object is only *ours* when we have it – when it exists for us as capital, or when it is directly possessed, eaten, drunk, worn, inhabited, etc., – in short, when it is *used* by us.

In the place of all physical and mental senses there has therefore come the sheer estrangement of all these senses, the sense of having. The human being had to be reduced to this absolute poverty in order that he might yield his inner wealth to the outer world.

History is not like some individual person, which uses men to achieve its ends. History is nothing but the actions of men in pursuit of their ends.

Perseus wore a magic cap down over his eyes and ears as a make-believe that there are no monsters.

Economists have a singular method of procedure. There are only two kinds of institutions for them, artificial and natural.

When the proletariat declares the dissolution of the hitherto existing world order, it merely declares the secret of its own existence, since it is in fact the dissolution of this order.

The bourgeoisie... has created enormous cities,

has greatly increased the urban population as compared with the rural, and has thus rescued a considerable part of the population from the idiocy of rural life. Just as it has made the country dependent on the towns, so it has made barbarian and semi-barbarian countries dependent on the civilised ones, nations of peasants on nations of bourgeois, the East on the West.

Up till now it has been thought that the growth of the Christian myths during the Roman Empire was possible only because printing was not yet invented. Precisely the contrary. The daily press and the telegraph, which in a moment spreads inventions over the whole earth, fabricate more myths (and the bourgeois cattle believe and enlarge upon them) in one day than could have formerly been done in a century.

It is one of the greatest misapprehensions to speak of free, human, social labour, of albour without private property. *"Labour"* by its very nature is unfree, unhuman, unsocial activity.

What is crucial in the true state is not the fact that every citizen has the chance to devote himself to the universal interest in the shape of a particular class, but the capacity of the universal class to be really universal, i.e. to be the class of every citizen.

The extremity of this bondage is that it is only as a worker that he continues to maintain himself as a physical subject, and that it is only as a physical subject that he is a worker.

The very same bourgeois mentality which extols the manufacturing division of labour, the life-long annexation of the worker to a partial operation, and the unconditional subordination of the detail worker to capital, extols them as an organisation of labour which increases productivity.

Man makes religion, religion does not make man. Religion is indeed man's self-consciousness and self-awareness as long as he has not found his feet in the universe.

As a matter of fact, the methods of primitive accumulation are anything but idyllic.

The forming of the five senses is a labour of the entire history of the world down to the present.

If you love without evoking love in return—that is, if your loving as loving does not produce reciprocal love; if through a living expression of yourself as a loving person you do not make yourself a loved person, then your love is impotent— a misfortune.

The more of himself man attributes to God, the less he has left in himself.

> The alienation of man thus appeared as the fundamental evil of capitalist society.

Freeman and slave, patrician and plebeian, lord and serf, guild-master and journeyman, in a word, oppressor and oppressed, stood in constant opposition to one another, carried on an uninterrupted, now hidden, now open fight, a fight that each time ended, either in a revolutionary reconstitution of society at large, or in the common ruin of the contending classes.

...which cannot be better described than by the cry of a Frenchman when it was planned to introduce a tax on dogs: 'Poor dogs! They want to treat you as human beings!

Men make their own history, but they do not make it as they please.

Finally, there came a time when everything that men had considered as inalienable became an object of exchange, of traffic and could be alienated.

Contempt for theory, art, history, and for man as an end in himself, which is contained in an abstract form in the Jewish religion, is the real, conscious standpoint, the virtue of the man of money. The species-relation itself, the relation between man and woman, etc., becomes an object of trade! The woman is bought and sold.

The essential difference between the various

economic forms of society, between, for instance, a society based on slave-labour, and one based on wage-labour, lies only in the mode in which this surplus-labour is in each case extracted from the actual producer, the labourer.

Nature does not produce on the one side owners of money or commodities, and on the other men possessing nothing but their own labour-power. This relation has no natural basis, neither is its social basis one that is common to all historical periods.

The bourgeoisie has stripped of its halo every occupation hitherto honoured and looked up to with reverent awe. It has converted the physician, the lawyer, the priest, the poet, the man of science, into its paid wage labourers.

The religious world is but the reflex of the real world.

The bourgeoisie cannot exist without constantly revolutionising the instruments of production, and thereby the relations of production, and with them the whole relations of society.

It compels all nations, on pain of extinction, to adopt
the bourgeois mode of production; it compels them to introduce
what it calls civilisation into their midst, i.e., to become bourgeois
themselves. In one word, it creates a world after its own image.

In general, the greater the productiveness of labour, the less is the labour time required for the production of an article, the less is the amount of labour crystallised in that article, and the less is its value.

The bourgeoisie has stripped of its halo every occupation hitherto honored and looked up to with reverent awe. It has converted the physician, the lawyer, the priest, the poet, the man of science, into its paid wage laborers.

He will then agree with Sismondi: "That capacity for labour ... is nothing unless it is sold".

The modern history of capital dates from the creation in the 16th century of a world-embracing commerce and a world-embracing market.

The executive of the modern State is but a committee for managing the common affairs of the whole bourgeoisie.

Not in vain does it [the proletariat] go through the stern but steeling school of labour. It is not a question of what this or that proletarian, or even the whole proletariat, at the moment regards as its aim. It is a question of what the proletariat is, and what, in accordance with this being, it will historically be compelled to do.

The immediate aim of the Communist is the same as that of all the other proletarian parties: formation of the proletariat into a class, overthrow of the bourgeois supremacy, conquest of political power by the proletariat.

The windmill gives you society with the feudal lord; the steam mill, society with the industrial capitalist.

Free trade: for the benefit of the working class. Protective duties: for the benefit of the working class. Prison Reform: for the benefit of the working class. This is the last word and the only seriously meant word of bourgeois Socialism. It is summed up in the phrase: the bourgeois is a bourgeois—for the benefit of the working class.

Social progress can be measured by the social position of the female sex.

It is a pure tautology to say that crises are provoked by a lack of effective demand or effective consumption. The capitalist system does not recognize any forms of consumer other than those who can pay, if we exclude the consumption of paupers and swindlers.

History is thorough, and passes through many phases when it bears an old figure to the grave. The last phase of a world historical figure is its comedy.

> **One must force** the frozen circumstances to dance, by singing to them their own melody.

This class has always to sacrifice a part of itself in order not to be wholly destroyed.

Theory becomes realized among a people only in so far as it represents the realization of that people's needs.

The lower strata of the middle class—the small tradespeople, shopkeepers, retired tradesmen generally, the handicraftsmen and peasants—all these sink gradually into the proletariat, partly because their diminutive capital does not suffice for the scale on which Modern Industry is carried on, and is swamped in the competition with the large capitalists, partly because their specialized skill is rendered worthless by the new methods of production. Thus the proletariat is recruited from all classes of the population.

“

All that is solid melts into air, all that is holy is profaned, and man is at last compelled to face with sober senses, his real conditions of life, and his relations with his kind.

”

If the State is to have reality as the ethical, self-conscious realization of spirit, it must be distinguished from the form of authority and faith.

The introduction of free competition is thus public declaration that from now on the members of society are unequal only to the extent that their capitals are unequal, that capital is the decisive power, and that therefore the capitalists, the bourgeoisie, have become the first class in society.

If conquest constitutes a natural right on the part of the few, the many have only to gather sufficient strength in order to acquire the natural right of reconquering what has been taken from them.

Every emancipation is a restoration of the human world and of human relationships to a man himself.

All fixed, fast-frozen relations, with their train of ancient and venerable prejudices and opinions, are swept away, all new-formed ones become antiquated before they can ossify.

In proportion as the exploitation of one individual by another is put an end to, the exploitation of one nation by another will also be put an end to. In proportion as the antagonism between classes within the nation vanishes, the hostility of one nation to another will come to an end.

There is only one way in which the murderous death agonies of the old society and the bloody birth throes of the new society can be shortened, simplified and concentrated, and that way is revolutionary terror.

The weapon of criticism cannot, of course, replace criticism of the weapon, material force must be overthrown by material force; but theory also becomes a material force as soon as it has gripped the masses.

The fact that labour is external to the worker, i.e., it does not belong to his intrinsic nature; that in his work, therefore he does not affirm himself but denies himself, does not feel content but unhappy, does not develop freely his physical and mental energy but mortifies his body and his mind. The worker therefore only feels himself outside his work, and in his work feels outside himself.

The head of this emancipation is philosophy; its heart is the proletariat. Philosophy cannot be realized without the abolition of the proletariat, the proletariat cannot abolish itself without realizing philosophy.

The brilliancy of Aristotle's genius is shown by this alone, that he discovered, in the expression of the value of commodities, a relation of equality. The peculiar conditions of the society in which he lived, alone prevented him from discovering what, "in truth," was at the bottom of this equality.

Under no pretext should arms and ammunition be surrendered; any attempt to disarm the workers must be frustrated, by force if necessary.

When the narrow bourgeois form has been peeled away, what is wealth, if not the universality of needs, capacities, enjoyments, productive powers etc., of individuals, produced in universal exchange?

Not only are they slaves of the bourgeois class, and of the bourgeois State; they are daily and hourly enslaved by the machine, by the over-looker, and, above all, by the individual bourgeois manufacturer himself.

The formula for the circuit of capital: M-C...P...C'-M', is the self-evident form of the circuit of capital only on the basis of already developed capitalist production, because it presupposes the availability of the class of wage-labourers in sufficient numbers throughout society.

The capitalist knows that all commodities, however scurvy they may look, or however badly they may smell, are in faith and in truth money, inwardly circumcised Jews, and what is more, a wonderful means whereby out of money to make more money.

For us the issue cannot be the alteration of private property but only its annihilation, not the smoothing over of class antagonisms but the abolition of classes not the improvement of the existing society but the foundation of a new one.

All mythology masters and dominates and shapes the forces of nature in and through the imagination; hence it disappears as soon as man gains mastery over the forces of nature.

Those professions which are not so much involved in life itself as concerned with abstract truths are the most dangerous for the young man whose principles are not yet firm and whose convictions are not yet strong and unshakeable. At the same time these professions may seem to be the most exalted if they have taken deep root in our hearts and if we are capable of sacrificing our lives and all endeavours for the ideas which prevail in them.

A class of labourers, who live only so long as they find work, and who find work only so long as their labour increases capital.

Franklin says, "war is robbery, commerce is generally cheating." If the transformation of merchants' money into capital is to be explained otherwise than by the producers being simply cheated, a long series of intermediate steps would be necessary, which, at present, when the simple circulation of commodities forms our only assumption, are entirely wanting.

This is what distinguishes the philosopher from the Christian. The Christian, in spite of logic, has only one incarnation of the Logos; the philosopher has never finished with incarnations.

There is a specter haunting Europe, the specter of Communism.

Modern bourgeois society with its relations of production, of exchange, and of property, a society that has conjured up such gigantic means of production and of exchange, is like the sorcerer, who is no longer able to control the powers of the nether world whom he has called up by his spells.

From each according to his ability, to each according to his needs!

The bourgeois period of history has to create the material basis of the new world — on the one hand universal intercourse founded upon the mutual dependency of mankind, and the means of that intercourse; on the other hand the development of the productive powers of man and the transformation of material production into a scientific domination of natural agencies. Bourgeois industry and commerce create these material conditions of a new world in the same way as geological revolutions have created the surface of the earth.

When the economists say that present-day relations – the relations of bourgeois production – are natural, they imply that these are the relations in which wealth is created and productive forces developed in conformity with the laws of nature. These relations therefore are themselves natural laws independent of the influence of time. They are eternal laws which must always govern society. Thus, there has been history, but there is no longer any.

Hitherto philosophers have had the solution of all riddles lying in their writing-desks, and the stupid, exoteric world had only to open its mouth for the roast pigeons of absolute knowledge to fly into it. Now philosophy has become mundane...

Money itself is the source of his gain, and is not used for the purposes for which it was invented.

On the basis of capitalist production, a new swindle with the wages of management develops in connection with joint-stock companies, in that, over and above the actual managing director, a number of governing and supervisory boards arise, for which management and supervision are in fact a mere pretext for the robbery of shareholders and their own enrichment.

The sudden expansion of the world market, the multiplication of commodities in circulation, the competition among the European nations for the seizure of Asiatic products and American treasures, the colonial system, all made a fundamental contribution towards shattering the feudal barriers to production.

A second and more practical, but less systematic, form of this Socialism sought to depreciate every revolutionary movement in the eyes of the working class, by showing that no mere political reform, but only a change in the material conditions of existence, in economic relations, could be of any advantage to them.

The class-struggles of the ancient world took the form chiefly of a contest between debtors and creditors, which in Rome ended in the ruin of the plebeian debtors. They were displaced by slaves. In the middle ages the contest ended with the ruin of the feudal debtors, who lost their political power together with the economic basis on which it was established. Nevertheless, the money relation of debtor and creditor that existed at these two periods reflected only the deeper-lying antagonism between the general economic conditions of existence of the classes in question.

Since the mass of the employed living labour is continually on the decline as compared to the mass of materialised labour set in motion by it, i.e., to the productively consumed means of production, it follows that the portion of living labour, unpaid and congealed in surplus-value, must also be continually on the decrease compared to the amount of value represented by the invested total capital. Since the ratio of the mass of surplus-value to the value of the invested total capital forms the rate of profit, this rate must constantly fall.

If we have chosen the position in life in which we can most of all work for mankind, no burdens can bow us down, because they are sacrifices for the benefit of all; then we shall experience no petty, limited, selfish joy, but our happiness will belong to millions, our deeds will live on quietly but perpetually at work, and over our ashes will be shed the hot tears of noble people.

From the standpoint of a higher economic form of society, private ownership of the globe by single individuals will appear quite as absurd as private ownership of one man by another. Even a whole society, a nation, or even all simultaneously existing societies taken together, are not the owners of the globe. They are only its possessors, its usufructuaries, and, like boni patres familias, they must hand it down to succeeding generations in an improved condition.

The less the skill and exertion of strength implied in manual labour, in other words, the more modern industry becomes developed, the more is the labour of men superseded by that of women. Differences of age and sex have no longer any distinctive social validity for the working class. All are instruments of labour, more or less expensive to use, according to their age and sex.

The realm of freedom actually begins only where labour which is determined by necessity and mundane considerations ceases.

The bourgeoisie, wherever it has got the upper

hand, has put an end to all feudal, patriarchal, idyllic relations. It has pitilessly torn asunder the motley feudal ties that bound man to his "natural superiors," and has left remaining no other nexus between man and man than naked self-interest, than callous "cash payment."

When, in the course of development, class distinctions have disappeared and all production has been concentrated in the hands of a vast association of the whole nation, the public power will lose its political character.

Every beginning is difficult, holds in all sciences.

I pre-suppose, of course, a reader who is willing to learn something new and therefore to think for himself.

The country that is more developed industrially only shows, to the less developed, the image of its own future.

The most violent, mean and malignant passions of the human breast, the Furies of private interest.

To discover the various use of things is the work of history.

Wherever the want of clothing forced them to it, the human race made clothes for thousands of years, without a single man becoming a tailor.

Every commodity is compelled to chose some other commodity for its equivalent.

Gold is now money with reference to all other commodities only because it was previously, with reference to them, a simple commodity.

The whole mystery of commodities, all the magic and necromancy that surrounds the products of labor as long as they take the form of commodities, vanishes therefore, so soon as we come to other forms of production.

There is a physical relation between physical things. But it is different with commodities.

Value, therefore, does not stalk about with a label describing what it is.

The law of gravity thus asserts itself when a house falls about our ears.

Under the ideal measure of values there lurks the hard cash.

We see then, commodities are in love with money, but "the course of true love never did run smooth".

> **Hence** money may be dirt, although dirt is not money.

Each piece of money is a mere coin, or means of circulation, only so long as it actually circulates.

Capital is money, capital is commodities. ... By virtue of it being value, it has acquired the occult ability to add value to itself. It brings forth living offspring, or, at the least, lays golden eggs.

And his money he cannot eat.

The way to Hell is paved with good intentions, and he might just as easily have intended to make money, without producing at all.

In every stock-jobbing swindle everyone knows that some time or other the crash must come, but every one hopes that it may fall on the head of his neighbour, after he himself has caught the shower of gold and placed it in safety.

The tool, as we have seen, is not exterminated by the machine.

Karl Marx

1818-1883

Further reading, works from Karl Marx:

Capital:
Capital, Volume I (1867)
Capital, Volume II (1885)
Capital, Volume III (1894)

Other works:
Scorpion and Felix (1837)
Oulanem (1839)
The Difference Between the Democritean and Epicurean
Philosophy of Nature (1841)
The Philosophical Manifesto of the Historical School of Law (1842)
Critique of Hegel's Philosophy of Right (1843)
On the Jewish Question (1843)
Notes on James Mill (1844)
Economic and Philosophic Manuscripts of 1844 (1927)
Theses on Feuerbach (1888)
The Poverty of Philosophy (1847)
Wage Labour and Capital (1847)
The Class Struggles in France, 1848–1850 (1850)
The Eighteenth Brumaire of Louis Napoleon (1852)
Grundrisse (1939)
A Contribution to the Critique of Political Economy (1859)
Theories of Surplus Value (three volumes, 1862)
Value, Price and Profit" (1865)
The Belgian Massacres (1869)
The Civil War in France (1871)
Critique of the Gotha Program (1875)
Mathematical manuscripts of Karl Marx (1968)

Marx and Engels:
The German Ideology (1845)
The Holy Family (1845)
The Communist Manifesto (1848)
The Civil War in the United States (1861)

Karl Marx

Quotes...

Receive the next Kindle Edition in the series FREE...

Sign up at

www.the**secret**libraries.com

The Secret Libraries

Published by The Secret Libraries
www.thesecretlibraries.com
Annotation and Artists Background by The Secret Libraries 2016

Paperback:
ISBN-13: 978-1540637178
ISBN-10: 1540637174

Copyright © 2016

For more information please find us at:

www.thesecretlibraries.com

Thank you for your purchase.

Printed in Great Britain
by Amazon

Vol.12 Karl Ma[rx]

by The Secret Librar[y]

This book provides a selected collection of 201 quotes from t[he]
works of Karl Ma[rx]

"The philosophers have only interpreted the world, in various wa[ys].
The point, however, is to change [it]"

"Let the ruling classes tremble at a Communistic revolution. The pr[o]
letarians have nothing to lose but their chains. They have a world [to]
win. Workingmen of all countries unite[!]"

"Go on, get out! Last words are for fools who haven't said enough[!]"
* The last words of Karl Marx (1818-188[3)]

Karl Marx

1818-188[3]

ISBN 9781540637178

90000 >

9 781540 637178